THE ILLUSTRATED
Meditations

THE ILLUSTRATED
Meditations

LIFE LESSONS FROM
Marcus Aurelius

INTRODUCED BY James Romm

ILLUSTRATED BY Joanna Lisowiec

RIVERSIDE PRESS

First published in 2025
by Riverside Press, an imprint of
UniPress Books Ltd
World's End Studios
London SW10 0RJ
United Kingdom

Translation of Marcus Aurelius
by George Long 1862,
updated for a modern audience

Introductions © James Romm 2025
Images © Joanna Lisowiec 2025
Copyright in the Work © UniPress Books Ltd
2025

The right of James Romm to be identified
as Author of the introductions in this Work has been
asserted in accordance with the Copyright, Designs
and Patents Act 1988

The right of Joanna Lisowiec to be identified
as Illustrator of this Work has been asserted
in accordance with the Copyright, Designs
and Patents Act 1988

ISBNs
Hardback: 978-1-917226-05-9
Ebook: 978-1-917226-06-6

All Rights Reserved. No part of this
publication may be reproduced, stored in a
retrieval system or transmitted in any form or
by any means, without prior permission in
writing from the publishers.
British Library Cataloguing-in-Publication
Data A catalogue record for this book is
available from the British Library.

Publisher: Jason Hook
Commissioning editor: Claire Collins
Designer: Alexandre Coco
Cover illustrations: Joanna Lisoweic
Printed in Slovenia
riversidepress.co.uk

CONTENTS

Introduction 7

Meditations...

on the Mind 13

on Living Well 35

on Community 57

on Nature 79

on the Gods 101

on Compassion 123

on Death 145

on Time 167

Further Reading 190 | **About the Contributors** 192

Introduction

Twice in the *Meditations* Marcus Aurelius, emperor of Rome from AD 161 to 180, deploys the metaphor of the dyeing of cloth. In the first of these passages (5.16), he tells himself to 'dye the soul with a continuous series of thoughts', the principles that will lead him towards a good life. In the second, he refers to the fact that, in his role as emperor or 'Caesar', he had the exclusive right to wear a robe dyed entirely purple, essentially a royal accoutrement. 'Take care to not become a Caesar,' he instructs himself, inventing a new Greek word (he writes in Greek, though Latin was his native language). Do not be 'dyed with that dye; it can happen'. He urges himself to follow the model of Antoninus, his adoptive father and predecessor as ruler, whom he considers a model of monarchic virtue (6.30; see page 118).

Here in these two metaphorical uses of dyeing, we see two sides of the man who today is often called by his first name, Marcus: his public role, that of ruler of a great part of the globe, and the innermost self he sought to improve by 'dyeing' it with the ideas he expresses in *Meditations*. His compilation of those ideas was never intended for publication; it served instead as a purely personal set of self-exhortations. Whenever he uses the pronoun 'you', or puts verbs into a second-person singular form, he is talking to himself, not to an imagined reader. Indeed the title of the work is sometimes given as *To Himself*, a more accurate description of its contents, perhaps, than *Meditations*, which became affixed to it only in the 17th century.

Dyeing in the ancient world required repeated dipping of cloth into dye, and *Meditations* is filled with repetition. Marcus comes back again and again to its central precepts, framing them in new ways or examining them from new angles. 'Your habitual thoughts will shape the character of your mind,' he tells himself in the first of his dyeing analogies, providing a good explanation of the goal of his work. His 'notebooks', as the twelve subdivisions of the work are sometimes termed, were his way of rehearsing the principles of his philosophical system. That system, inherited from the Greeks of the 3rd century BC by way of Roman intermediaries, is called Stoicism, after the Painted Stoa, a colonnade in Athens where its founding father, Zeno of Citium, used to instruct his disciples.

In his notebooks Marcus allows himself to roam freely among a wide range of topics, as though addressing day by day whatever was most on his mind. The current volume selects from this sometimes confusing jumble a small set of crucial entries, then groups them into eight thematically organised chapters. Readers will find an inviting, and beautifully illustrated, pathway into the *Meditations*, arranged so as to give an overview of Marcus' system of belief. That system, Stoic philosophy, was already centuries old when he wrote and is now many times older; yet, as this collection demonstrates, the principles Marcus took from it are still as potent as ever, teaching us how to *live* and not merely to *be*.

The tenets of Marcus' Stoicism will be explored, one by one, in the introductions to the chapters that follow, but a broad outline can be given here. For the Stoics, the good life is a life in harmony with Nature, for Nature is thoroughly rational and benign, the expression of the rational force that controls the larger cosmos. That force can be conceived of as the gods or as God, as Mind, or as *Logos*, a multi-layered Greek word that includes ideas of reason, speech and thought. Our human capacity for reason has been bestowed by this benevolent force, bringing us closer to divinity than any other species. To follow its promptings unswervingly would make us even more godlike, as we are meant to be.

What does our reason prompt us to do, as we go about a largely unreasonable world? Above all, to act virtuously, for virtue is in accord with the divine plan for the cosmos. We are social creatures who depend on bonds of fellowship for survival, since we lack the assets – claws, fangs, tough hides and the like – that protect other species. Our uniquely social existence requires that we treat one another well, so virtuous behaviour is in accord with Mind and with Nature. We belong to a human community, so everything that benefits that community also benefits us. False opinions, however, lead us to pursue private objectives – pleasure, or wealth, or fame – as sources of happiness. Stoics consider such things 'indifferent' in that they conduce neither to virtue nor vice, and therefore do not affect our happiness in any real sense.

Along with the problem of false opinions, Stoic practice also means coping with the *phantasiai* or 'impressions' that are constantly streaming into our souls. Sights or smells may arouse our desire for pleasure, things we hear – for example, insults – may stimulate our anger, or pain felt by our nervous system may provoke fear. These emotional responses can overwhelm our rational minds, if we allow them to do so. We must instead put our reactions on hold and ask the only question that matters: 'Will this hinder my capacity for reason and virtue?' If the answer is no, we'd have no reason to dread even attacks of wild beasts or slanders hurled at us by an entire nation, Marcus maintains. Such apparently miserable experiences are actually indifferent, in that they do not make us any more or less virtuous.

There's far more to orthodox Stoicism than what has been summarised here, but these are the themes that Marcus is most concerned with in *Meditations*, the rosary beads of his mind. He recurs to them over and over, as though determined not to let go of the insights he has gained. The earnestness of his project is what makes it compelling; his writing takes energy from the gravity of his quest. There are few moments of levity in *Meditations*, and nothing ironic or insincere. Marcus never hides behind an authorial mask, as other ancient philosophic writers, Plato and Seneca among them, often do. He is writing only for and to himself, a circumstance that makes his prose uniquely authentic and genuine.

How did such a private text, in essence a personal journal, come to be preserved such that we can read it today? That question, like many concerning *Meditations*, is difficult to answer. We don't know for certain when Marcus began writing the work or when he stopped. Two of the twelve notebooks, numbers 2 and 3, bear headings indicating the places they were composed, in both cases military outposts on Rome's northern frontier. Marcus was on campaign in this region during the early 170s, fighting Germanic tribes that were making incursions, so it can be assumed he wrote those parts of *Meditations* at that time. He was still on campaign in the north when he died in AD 180; presumably he had the notebooks with him and some quick-witted underling ensured they were not discarded.

The idea that Marcus was engaged in a gruelling series of wars, designed to fend off threats to Rome's borders, when he wrote *Meditations* has added to the stature of the work and, for some readers, augmented its power to inspire. Two widely viewed American films, *The Fall of the Roman Empire* (1964) and *Gladiator* (2000), portray Marcus as a stolid, stalwart commander, defending the empire despite the toll of advancing age. Both films have also highlighted, for readers of *Meditations*, the pathos of Marcus' position at the edge of a historical precipice. He was the last of the 'five good emperors', a series that had begun more than eight decades before his death, and his successor, his debauched son Commodus, brought that long era of stability to an end.

A weary man in his fifties, a sage who turns warrior out of a sense of duty, all the while knowing his heir may undo all he has done – it's a compelling portrait, at least in the way Hollywood has constructed it. But we do not need a biography to gain inspiration from *Meditations*; its teachings transcend time and place. Indeed, if the work had been handed down without the name of its author, only a very few passages, such as the praise of Antoninus, would allow us to guess that the wealthiest, most powerful man in the world had composed it.

Few of us need worry about becoming 'Caesarised', but all of us face, every day, challenges to the qualities that make us fully human: our rationality, our benevolence, our capacity for virtuous action. To meet those challenges requires constant effort, a dyeing of the mind by repeated dipping. The task is never finished, but the rewards are enormous and within the reach of every spiritual striver. If Marcus could succeed – and it seems, to judge by *Meditations*, that he did – then so can we. ❧

CHAPTER 1
Meditations on the Mind

Shakespeare's Hamlet is speaking like a Stoic when he says 'There's nothing good or bad but thinking makes it so.' To Stoics like Marcus, the opinions formed by the undisciplined mind are the source of most human unhappiness. If we believe that wealth or status, or even the love of our nearest and dearest, hold the key to our happiness, we'll be tormented by the lack or loss of these things. We must dye the soul, as Marcus puts it in one of his most memorable phrases (5.16), by constantly rehearsing the truths in which our happiness lies: that Nature intends us to be guided by our reason, to act virtuously, and to benefit our community. 'The good for a reasonable being is society,' Marcus writes, in a list of the 'dyes' to which our minds should recur.

False opinions are spawned both by the influence of others on our sense of self – the 'clapping of hands' and the 'clapping of tongues' (6.16) – and by our mistaken reliance on our perceptions of the physical world, which is constantly changing and filled with illusions. 'The universe is transformation; life is opinion,' Marcus writes (4.3), implying that the second proposition arises out of the first. He shares with the followers of Plato the idea that knowledge of the good cannot come from our senses. He urges that we look for a divine or guardian spirit inside ourselves, which 'has detached itself from the persuasions of sensation, submitted itself to the gods, and which cares for humanity' (3.6), then allow that force to occupy our entire soul.

Despite his conviction about the damaging effect of wrong opinion, Marcus expresses remarkable compassion for those who had not 'seen the light'. In 2.1 he asserts, again following the lead of Plato, that wrong action arises not from an evil or malevolent nature, but from 'ignorance of what is good and evil'. That thesis leads him to treat his fellow human beings with compassion even when their actions offend him, for 'they are kin to me' in the sense of having a rational mind bestowed, like his, by divinity. It also makes him impervious to their slights or insults, for by seeing these as the product of ignorance, he disarms his own sense of having been insulted.

To allow oneself to be swayed by impressions and opinions, rather than putting one's reasoning mind in control, is to make oneself a puppet dancing on a string, or to behave like a herd animal that breathes and feeds automatically (6.16). Humankind is distinct from the rest of the animal kingdom, and certainly from plants, by our capacity for rational thought. Because of this capacity, Marcus believes, we stand closer to the gods in the great cosmic hierarchy than to the unreasoning creatures below us. If we fully trust in the promptings of the mind, we will achieve harmony with the gods, the most sublime form of happiness and peace. ❈

Consider that everything is opinion, and that opinion is something you can control. Choose to change your opinion, and like a mariner who has passed choppy headland waters, you will find a calm, waveless bay

BOOK XII, MEDITATION 22

As physicians have their tools ready for cases which suddenly require their skill, so you should have your principles ready for the understanding of divine and worldly things

BOOK III, MEDITATION 13

Meditations on the Mind

Begin each morning by saying to yourself: I will encounter people who are nosy, ungrateful, arrogant, deceitful, envious and unsocial. All these things are so because of these people's ignorance of what is good and evil. But I have seen the nature of the good that is beautiful, and of the bad that is ugly, and the nature of such people who do wrong. They are kin to me, not as blood relatives, but as people participating in the same intelligence and the same portion of divinity as me. And so I cannot be injured by them, for they cannot fix on me what is ugly, nor can I be angry with or hate my kin.

BOOK II, MEDITATION 1

Above all do not distract or strain yourself, but be free, and look at things as an individual, as a human being, as a citizen, as a mortal. But always remember these two ideas: firstly, that simple objects do not touch the soul, for they are external and immovable. Our sufferings come only from our opinions, which are formed within ourselves. And secondly, that all these things which you see are in a constant state of change and will one day cease to exist. Constantly bear in mind how many of these changes you yourself have already witnessed. The universe is transformation; life is opinion.

BOOK IV, MEDITATION 3

I have often wondered how it is that every person loves themselves more than all the rest of humanity, yet sets less value on their own opinion of themselves than on the opinion of others. If a god or a wise teacher was to one day meet someone, and make them think of nothing and wish for nothing which they would not express out loud as soon as they had thought of it, they would not endure it, not even for a single day. We have so much more respect for what our neighbours may think of us than for what we think ourselves.

BOOK XII, MEDITATION 4

Meditations on the Mind

Your habitual thoughts will shape the character of your mind, for our souls are dyed the colour of our thoughts

BOOK V, MEDITATION 16

Return to your senses; just as when you have roused yourself from sleep and learned it was only a dream that troubled you, in your waking hours, look at the things around you as if they were dreams

BOOK VI, MEDITATION 31

Meditations on the Mind

Things themselves cannot touch the soul, not in the least degree. They do not have admission to the soul, nor can they turn or move it. The soul turns and moves itself alone, and whatever judgements it feels are proper, it sees the things which present themselves to it in accordance with those judgements.

BOOK V, MEDITATION 19

My soul, will you never be good, simple, one and naked, more manifest than the body which surrounds you? Will you never enjoy an affectionate and contented disposition? Will you never be full and free of want, longing for nothing more, nor desiring anything, either animate or inanimate, for the enjoyment of pleasures? Nor yet desiring longer enjoyment, or place, or pleasant climate, or good company? Will you instead be satisfied with your present condition, and pleased with all that you have? Will you convince yourself that you have everything, that what you have comes from the gods and that all is well for you? And that it will be well whatever will please them, and whatever they will give for the conservation of the perfect living being, the good, just and beautiful, which generates and holds together all things, and contains and embraces all things which are dissolved for the production of other like things?

BOOK X, MEDITATION 1

Acquire and constantly attend to the contemplative way of seeing how all things change into one another: exercise yourself about this part of philosophy. For nothing is better adapted to produce magnanimity. A person who achieves this has put off the body and sees that they must – no one knows how soon – go away, leaving everyone and everything here. They become entirely just in all their actions, and in everything else that happens, they resign themselves to the universal Nature. But as to what any person might say, think or do against them, they never even think of it, being straightforwardly contented with these two things: with acting justly, and being satisfied with everything that is now assigned to them.

BOOK X, MEDITATION 11

Retire into yourself. The rational principle has this nature; it is content with itself when it does what is fair, and in this way it secures tranquillity

BOOK VII, MEDITATION 28

Nothing elevates the mind so much as being able to examine, methodically and truly, every object and experience which is presented to you in life

BOOK III, MEDITATION 11

Meditations on the Mind

Transpiration in plants is not something to value, nor is breathing in domesticated animals or wild beasts, nor is the receiving of impressions by the appearances of things. These are all the same as being moved by desires as puppets are moved by strings, or assembling in herds, or being nourished by food; this is just like the act of eliminating the waste part of that same food. What then is of value? To be received with clapping hands? No. Neither should we value the clapping of tongues, for praise which comes from the many is a clapping of tongues. Suppose then that you have given up this worthless thing

called fame – what remains that is worth valuing? In my opinion, this: to both move and restrain yourself in conformity to your proper constitution, to which end all employments and arts lead. For every art aims at this: that the thing should be adapted to the work for which it has been made. Thus the vine-planter who looks after the vine, the horse-breaker who looks after the horse and the dog trainer who trains the dog, they all seek this end. The education and the teaching of youth aim at something; in this then is the value of education and teaching. And if this is well, you will not seek anything else. Will you not cease to value many other things too? Then you will neither be free, nor sufficient for your own happiness, nor without passion. For of necessity, you must be envious, jealous and suspicious of those who might take away those things, and plot against those who have that which is valued by you. Of necessity a person who wants any of these things must be in a disturbed state; and they must often find fault with the gods too. But to reverence and honour your own mind will make you content with yourself, and in harmony with society, and in agreement with the gods, that is, praising all that they give and have ordered.

BOOK VI, MEDITATION 16

CHAPTER 2

Meditations on Living Well

Marcus quotes the aphorism 'everything which happens, happens justly' with approval in *Meditations*. Like other Stoics, he believed that the universe was ordered by a benign divinity, so everything that occurs within it, even in our individual lives, belongs to a chain of cause and effect that is largely predetermined. We have no control over much of what happens to us, but we *can* control our response. If we accept the goodness and rightness of what takes place, on the principle that it all belongs to the chain, we won't feel troubled even at apparent misfortune. The Latin phrase *amor fati*, 'love of one's fate', is sometimes used to describe this kind of acceptance; Friedrich Nietzsche devised the phrase but Marcus says something similar to it at 7.57 below, 'Love only that which happens to you and which is spun with the thread of destiny.'

Embracing one's fate as a thread of the cosmic web is one of several ways in which our minds provide solace for, or refuge from, life's vicissitudes. The Stoics imagined the rational mind as an 'inner citadel' to which we can retreat, just as a population under attack might retreat inside a fortress. Marcus uses a different metaphor below (4.49), that of a rocky cliff face battered by waves, to express the idea that our habits of mind can make us invulnerable. He also compares the sanctuary offered by the mind to a salve applied as a cure for an ailment (5.9), and contrasts it with the vacation homes sought by the wealthy (4.3) – places that give only superficial refreshment.

The steps by which inner peace is achieved are not easy, as Marcus understands, but we can take strength from knowing they are certain to succeed. He lays out a kind of programme at 3.12. First and foremost, we must follow 'right reason', the divine part of our natures, unswervingly, ignoring the things that might cause distraction. In many places Marcus terms this element *hegemonikon*, or 'that which directs or controls', the soul's executive function. The gods have programmed this part of us for virtuous thought and action, so if we give it full sway, we will become virtuous and therefore, in Stoic terms, happy.

Marcus allows for the possibility that he will not always obey 'right reason', or that he will lose his commitment to virtue after having attained it (5.9, 10.8). In Stoic terms he sees himself as a striver or seeker rather than a *sapiens*, 'sage', one who has attained perfect harmony with reason and Nature. What's essential is to regain equilibrium quickly once one has lost it, if necessary by withdrawing into some 'nook' – a mental, not a physical, place of retreat. The constant recommitment to virtue and reason imparts 'a new life' and a new kind of self (10.8), whereas to continue along old paths, obeying impulses or seeking pleasure and fame, makes one like the gladiator who goes back to the arena, day after day, to be attacked by wild beasts. ❦

While you live, while it is in your power, be good

BOOK IV, MEDITATION 17

Be like the cliff face against which waves continually crash, but which stands firm and tames the fury of the water around it

BOOK IV, MEDITATION 49

Meditations on Living Well

Do not be disgusted, discouraged or dissatisfied if you do not succeed in doing everything according to right principles. Rather, when you have failed, return back again, and be content if the majority of what you do is consistent with the nature of humanity. Love that to which you return. Do not come back to philosophy as if she were a master, but be like those who have sore eyes and apply a bit of sponge and balm, or as another applies a plaster, or as another drenches with water. In this way, you will succeed in obeying reason, and you will repose in it.

BOOK V, MEDITATION 9

Love only that which happens to you and which is spun with the thread of destiny. What could be more suitable? In everything that happens, think of people who previously experienced the same things; how they were vexed, disbelieving, fault-finding. And where are those people now? Nowhere. Why then do you choose to act in the same way? Why not leave such agitations, which are foreign to nature, to those who either cause them or are moved by them? Why are you not completely committed to the right way of making use of the things which happen to you? For then you will use them well, and they will be a material for you to work on. Attend only to yourself and resolve to be good in every act you undertake.

BOOK VII, MEDITATION 57

Meditations on Living Well

If then, you have truly seen how things are, forget wondering how you will seem to others, and be content if you can live the rest of your life as your nature wills. Observe what this involves and let nothing else distract you. You have experienced many wanderings without finding happiness anywhere; not in syllogisms, nor in wealth, nor in reputation, nor in indulgence; nowhere. Where then can it be found? In doing what humanity's nature requires. And how is this achieved? Through having principles, from which come one's affects and actions. What principles? Those which relate to good and bad: the belief that there is nothing good for a person which does not make them just, temperate, brave and free; and that there is nothing bad which does not do the contrary.

BOOK VIII, MEDITATION 1

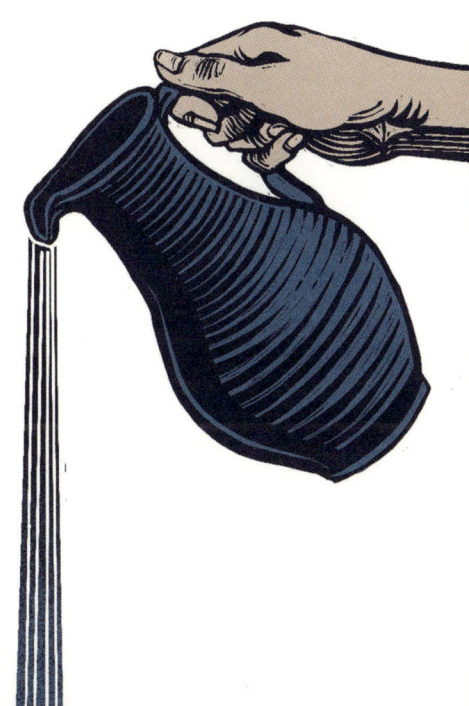

Look inside of yourself. There is a fountain of good there, and it will flow forever, if you will only look for it

BOOK VII, MEDITATION 59

Know that this place is like any other, and that all things here are the same as they would be on top of a mountain, or by the seashore, or wherever else you might choose to be

BOOK X, MEDITATION 23

Meditations on Living Well

Every moment, think steadily as a Roman and as a person, to do what you must with perfect and simple dignity, with affection, freedom and justice, and give yourself relief from all other thoughts. And you will achieve relief, if you make every act of your life as if it were your last, laying aside all carelessness and passionate aversion to the commands of reason, and all hypocrisy, self-love and discontent with the portion which has been given to you.

BOOK II, MEDITATION 5

If you work at that which is before you, following right reason seriously, vigorously, calmly, without allowing anything else to distract you, but keeping your divine part pure, as if you were bound to return it immediately – if you hold to this, expecting nothing, fearing nothing, but satisfied with your present activity according to Nature, and with heroic truth in every word and sound which you utter, you will live happily. And no one will be able to prevent this.

BOOK III, MEDITATION 12

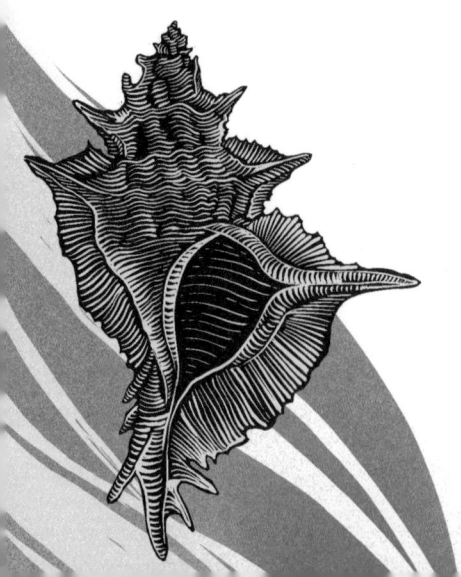

Meditations on Living Well

People seek retreats for themselves, houses in the country, or by the seashore, or in the mountains. You too might desire such escapes very much. And yet this is a mark of the most unthinking kind of person, for it is in anyone's power to retreat into their own mind, whenever they wish. There is nowhere with more quiet or more freedom from trouble than one's own soul, particularly when one has thoughts which inspire immediate and perfect tranquillity. And, I declare, tranquillity is nothing more than the good ordering of the mind. And so, give yourself this retreat constantly, and renew yourself.

BOOK IV, MEDITATION 3

Think less of what you lack than of what you have. In some instances, perhaps you already have the very best of something. Then reflect how eagerly you would wish for these things now, if they were not yours already. At the same time, however, take care that you do not, through being so pleased, accustom yourself to overvalue them, so as to be upset if you were ever to lose them.

BOOK VII, MEDITATION 27

Everything that occurs either happens in a way that you are formed by nature to be able to bear, or you are not. If, then, something happens to you that you are able to bear, do not complain, but bear it as you are formed to do. But if it happens in such a manner that you cannot bear, do not complain, for the thing will perish after it has consumed you. Remember, however, that you are formed by nature to bear everything, in that it depends on your own opinion to make something endurable and tolerable, by thinking that it is either in your interest or your duty to do this.

BOOK X, MEDITATION 3

Affected honesty is like a crooked stick; nothing is more disgraceful than the false friendship of wolves. Avoid this most of all

BOOK XI, MEDITATION 15

All that you wish to reach one day by way of a winding route you can have now, if you do not refuse it to yourself. Take no notice of the past, trust the future to providence and direct the present only to piety and justice

BOOK XII, MEDITATION 1

Show these attributes then, which are altogether in your power: sincerity, gravity, hard work, aversion to pleasure, contentment with your portion and with few things, benevolence, frankness, simplicity, freedom from trifling, magnanimity. Do you not see how many qualities you could immediately exhibit, in which there is no excuse of natural incapacity and unfitness, and yet you remain voluntarily below the mark? Or are you compelled through being defectively furnished by nature to murmur, to be stingy, to flatter, to find fault with your poor body, to try to please others, to show off, and to be so restless in your mind? No, by the gods! And yet, you might have been delivered from these things long ago. Only if in truth you are rather slow and dull of comprehension – but if that is so you must exert yourself in that way too, not neglecting it or taking pleasure in your dullness.

BOOK V, MEDITATION 5

When you have earned these names: good, modest, true, rational, composed and magnanimous, take care that you do not change them, and reclaim them quickly if you should lose them. Remember that the term 'rational' means a discriminating attention to everything and freedom from neglect, and that composure is the voluntary acceptance of what is assigned to you by fate. Remember also that magnanimity is the elevation of intelligence above the pleasurable or painful sensations of the flesh and also worthless fame, death and all such things. If then, you maintain your possession of these qualities, without desiring to be recognised as such by others, you will become another person and will enter a new life. For to continue as you have until now, to be torn in pieces and defiled, is the character of a very foolish person and one overfond of their life, like those half-devoured fighters with wild beasts, who though covered in wounds and gore, still intreat to be kept to the following day, though they will be exposed in the same way to the same claws and bites. Therefore, take possession of these names, and if you can abide in them, abide as if you were removed to paradise. But if you perceive that you cannot maintain your hold on them, go courageously to some quiet place where you can regain them.

BOOK X, MEDITATION 8

CHAPTER 3

Meditations on Community

Aristotle famously declared that human beings are by nature 'political', that is, formed for aggregation into a *polis* or city-state. By the time Stoicism emerged, in the generation after Aristotle's, the boundaries of the city-state had begun to dissolve as the conquests of Alexander the Great created a vastly larger entity, an empire spanning much of the world then known. The original Stoics, the Greeks of Alexander's era, developed ideas about the unity of all peoples that suited this historical evolution, and those ideas evolved further in imperial Rome. The notion that all humanity shares a common affiliation, that we are 'citizens of the world', was deeply congenial to the Roman project and to Marcus' role as monarch over the peoples of three continents. The contradictions between this ideal and the reality of Marcus' reign, which included a series of wars against tribes dwelling north of the Danube, are only glancingly noted in *Meditations*.

In 4.4 below Marcus derives our communal impulse from our innate capacity for reason, which is to say, from the gods (or from God – at 7.9 he asserts, as the Stoics in general did, the singular nature of the divine). Reason tells us what to do or what not to do, and thus gives rise to law, which Marcus considers a 'common' or universal set of principles (downplaying the ways in which laws can differ from one society to another). Since all humanity shares this 'common' law, we all belong to a single state that is coextensive with the *cosmos*, a Greek word here translated as 'world', but which also sometimes includes the visible universe and which carries the additional meaning 'orderly array'. With this one term, Marcus links together the heavens, the earth and the whole of human society as parallel manifestations of divine reason.

Marcus acknowledges that other creatures besides human beings form communities; he mentions bees and cattle at 9.9, asserting that these animals too must have 'souls' that bring them together. Higher degrees of reason lead to higher aspirations – in the case of humans, 'political communities and friendships, and families and meetings of people; and in wars, treaties and armistices'. But humans have also managed to disregard their natural impulse towards unity and fellowship. 'See, then, what now takes place,' Marcus writes, perhaps in reference to the wars he was engaged in at the time he was writing; 'intelligent animals have forgotten this mutual desire and inclination.' He remains confident that 'nature', the source of our drive towards community, will win out in the end.

For Stoics like Marcus, the idea of a unified world-state impels us towards acts of kindness and benevolence. In 7.13 Marcus uses a play on words to make his point: we must consider ourselves a *melos* or 'limb' of the collective human body, not a *meros* or 'part' that can exist on its own. To see things that way would lead us to 'love humanity from the heart' and to understand that in doing good to others we also do good to ourselves. ❧

It is possible to live in a palace without wanting uniforms, torches, statues or other such trappings of pretension. It is possible to behave very like an ordinary citizen without being meaner in thought or remiss in action as a ruler

BOOK I, MEDITATION 17

Meditations on Community

All things are so separated and diffused and sympathetic

BOOK IV, MEDITATION 27

Meditations on Community

Whatever I do, either alone or with other people, should focus solely on that which is useful and well suited to society.

How many who once enjoyed fame have been given up to oblivion, and how many who once celebrated the fame of others have long been dead?

Do not be ashamed to be helped for it is your business to do your duty, like a soldier in the assault on a town. What if, because of an injury, you cannot mount the battlements alone, but the help of another makes it possible?

Do not let future things disturb you. You will come to them, if it is necessary, having with you the same reason which you now use for present things.

All things are implicated with one another, and the bond is holy; almost nothing is unconnected to anything else. For things have been co-ordinated, and they combine to form the universe. There is one universe made up of all things, one god who pervades those things, one substance, one law, one common reason in all intelligent animals and one truth; if indeed there is also one perfection for all intelligent beings who participate in reason.

Meditations on Community

Everything material soon disappears in the substance of the whole; and everything formal is very soon taken back into the universal reason, and the memory of everything is very soon overwhelmed in time.

To the rational animal the same act is according to nature and according to reason.

Stand up, or be held up.

Just like with the limbs of bodies which are united in one, so it is with rational beings which exist separately, for they been designed for cooperation. And this will be clear to you, if you often say to yourself that I am a limb (or melos) of the system of rational beings. But if you instead say you are a part (or meros), you do not yet love humanity from your heart, goodness does not yet delight you for its own sake, you still do it merely as a thing of propriety, and not yet as a goodness to yourself.

BOOK VII, MEDITATION 5–13

Meditations on Community

Some people, when they have helped another, note that they are owed a favour. Some privately think of the person they have helped as their debtor. But some people are like vines which produce grapes; they seek nothing once they have produced their fruit

BOOK V, MEDITATION 6

So far as I am myself, my city, my country, is Rome. But as a human being, it is the world. The things that benefit these places can only benefit me

BOOK VI, MEDITATION 44

All things which participate in anything common, move towards that which is the same as themselves. That which is earthy turns towards the earth, everything which is liquid flows together, and everything which is aerial does the same. To keep like things apart something is required, like the application of force. Fire moves upwards because of the elemental fire, but it is so ready to be kindled together with other fire, that any somewhat dry substance is easily ignited, because there is less within it which counters ignition. Accordingly then, everything which participates in the common intelligent nature gravitates towards that which is the same as itself. For so much as it is superior in comparison with all other things, it is also more ready to mingle with and to be fused with that which is its kin. Accordingly, among animals devoid of reason we find swarms of bees and herds of cattle, and the nurture of young birds,

Meditations on Community

and in a manner, love; for even animals have souls. That power which brings them together is seen to exert itself more, and in a way that has never been observed in plants, stones or trees. But in rational animals there are political communities and friendships, and families and meetings of people; and in wars, treaties and armistices. And in the things which are still superior, even though they are separated from one another, unity in a manner exists, as with the stars. Thus, the ascent to the higher degree is able to produce a sympathy even in things which are separated. See then, what now takes place. For only intelligent animals have forgotten this mutual desire and inclination, and only in them is the property of flowing together not seen. But still though men strive to avoid this union, they are caught and held by it, for their nature is too strong for them.

BOOK IX, MEDITATION 9

Anyone who talks about humanity should look at earthly things as if from above; assemblies, armies, agricultural labours, marriages, treaties, births, deaths, courts of justice, feasts, lamentations, markets; a mixture of all things and an orderly combination of contraries

BOOK VII, MEDITATION 48

Meditations on Community

We are made for cooperation, like feet, like hands, like eyelids, like rows of upper and lower teeth. To act against one another is contrary to nature; and it is acting against one another to be vexed and to turn away.

BOOK II, MEDITATION 1

If our intellectual part is common, then so is our reason, and we are rational beings. If this is so, we also share the reason which commands what we may and may not do. If this is so, there is a common law and we are all fellow citizens. If this is so, we are members of a political community, and the world is in a manner a state. For of what other political community will anyone say that the whole human race are members? And from there, from this common political community comes also our intellectual and reasoning faculty and our capacity for law. For where else could they come from? Just as my earthly part is a portion given to me from earth, and that which is watery comes from another element, and that which is hot and fiery comes from some other source (for nothing comes from or returns to nothing), so the intellectual part also comes from some source.

BOOK IV, MEDITATION 4

Meditations on Community

When you are troubled by something, you have forgotten all of the following: that everything happens according to the universal Nature; that someone else's wrongful act is nothing to you; that everything which happens, always happened and will happen again so everywhere; and how close the kinship is between one person and the whole human race, for it is a community, not of blood or family, but of intelligence. And you have forgotten these things too: that everyone's intelligence is a god, and is an efflux of the deity; that nothing is a person's own, but that one's own child, body and even one's own soul came from the deity. Lastly, you have forgotten these things too: that everything is opinion; and that everyone lives the present time only, and loses only this.

BOOK XII, MEDITATION 26

A branch cut off from its neighbouring branch is inevitably cut off from the whole tree also. So too a person, when they are separated from another, falls from the whole social community

BOOK XI, MEDITATION 8

CHAPTER 4

Meditations on Nature

Two of the Greek founders of Stoicism, Zeno and Cleanthes, are said to have defined the goal of their philosophy as 'living in accord with Nature'. By 'Nature' they meant something far larger than the great outdoors. In the Stoic view the entire cosmos constitutes a living organism, of which all earthly creatures, even 'the little plants, the little birds, the ants, the spiders and bees' (5.1), are parts, like the cells of a body. The mind that animates this vast organism is the *Logos* or divine Reason that pervades it and gives it order. So living in harmony with Nature means also following Reason as one's guide, and accepting the role that has been assigned by the cosmic intelligence.

Marcus is certain that this ensouled organism called Nature is entirely good, so that everything its parts undergo must also be good. At 10.7 he rejects both the idea that Nature allows any of its parts to be harmed, and that anything other than Nature could be at work on those parts; therefore every natural process is beneficial. Even the cyclical destruction of the universe itself, a Stoic doctrine Marcus alludes to at the end of 10.7 ('whether this at certain points is consumed by fire'), should be seen as a benefit, for the world is refreshed and cleansed by the fires that consume it. A new world arises after the conflagration, every bit as good as the old and perhaps even identical with it (see 9.28, page 110).

The conviction that Nature is wholly good reinforces the Stoic principle of *amor fati* or embrace of one's fate. Marcus asserts at 10.6 that Nature 'cannot be compelled ... to generate anything harmful to itself'. That thought leads him to be 'content with everything that happens', or to 'receive [that which happens] and refer it to the gods and the source of all things'. Only a fool would ask why things like thorny briars exist (8.50), for the question implies that thorns are less valuable than flowers. But by the same token, only a fool takes delight in 'roses in spring and fruit in summer' (4.44); such things are just as indifferent, in regard to our capacity for virtue, as are the things most people regard as evils.

Marcus recurs several times in *Meditations* to the fact that Nature is always changing; at 10.7 he even redefines death as a process of change. Since change is inherent in Nature, there's no reason to fear deterioration or death; the elements that make up the living body are simply disaggregating, not disappearing (2.17). Marcus was fond of the early Greek philosopher Heraclitus, whom he quotes on this point: 'The death of earth is to become water, the death of water is to become air, and the death of air is to become fire' (4.46, page 165). From Heraclitus he takes the metaphor of the flowing stream (6.15), an image of earthly existence as an endless series of changes. In vain do we clutch at the objects borne by the stream, for they are soon carried past us, never to return. ❖

If there is no harm to the elements themselves as they continually change forms, why should any person be apprehensive about the change or dissolution of elements? This change is according to Nature, and nothing evil is in accordance with Nature

BOOK II, MEDITATION 17

Figs gape open when they are ripe, and in ripe olives, the fact of their being close to rottenness adds a peculiar beauty to the fruit

BOOK III, MEDITATION 3

Everything which happens is as familiar and well known as roses in spring and fruit in summer; like disease, death, slander and treachery, and whatever else fools allow to delight or vex them

BOOK IV, MEDITATION 44

Don't you see the little plants, the little birds, the ants, the spiders and the bees, all working together to order the various parts of the universe?

BOOK V, MEDITATION 1

In this flowing stream then, where there can be no lingering, what is there of all the things which hurry by which anyone should prize?

BOOK VI, MEDITATION 15

That which is not good for the hive, neither is it good for the bee

BOOK VI, MEDITATION 54

Meditations on Nature

Nature is involved in everything, as much at the end as the beginning and continuance. Just like a person who throws up a ball, what good is it for the ball to be thrown up, or harm for it to come down, or even to have fallen? And what good is it to a bubble while it holds together, or what harms when it is burst? The same may be said of a candle also.

Turn it inside out, and see what kind of thing it is; including when it is old or diseased.

Short-lived are both the praise-giver and the praised, and the person who remembers and the one who is remembered. And all this is in a nook of this part of the world; and not even here does everyone agree, no, not any one with himself: and the whole earth too is a tiny point.

Attend to the matter which is before you, whether it is an opinion or an act or a word.

You suffer what you suffer justly: for you choose rather to become good tomorrow than to be good today.

Am I doing something? I do it with reference to the good of humanity. Does something happen to me? I receive it and refer it to the gods, and the source of all things, from which all that happens is derived.

Such as bathing appears to you – oil, sweat, dirt, filthy water, everything disgusting – so is every part of life and everything.

BOOK VIII, MEDITATIONS 20–26

Meditations on Nature

Hindrance to the perceptions of sense and desire are evils to the animal nature. There are similar evils to the constitution of plants. It follows then that hindrance to the intelligence is an evil to the intelligent nature. So, apply all of this to yourself. Does pain or sensuous pleasure affect you? The senses will look to that. Has an obstacle opposed you in your efforts towards a particular goal? If indeed you were making this effort absolutely (unconditionally, without reservation) certainly that is an evil to you, as a rational animal. But if you consider the usual course of things, you have not yet been injured or even impeded. The things which are proper to the understanding however, no other person is used to impede, for neither fire, iron, tyrant nor abuse touches it in any way. When it has been made a sphere, it continues a sphere.

BOOK VIII, MEDITATION 41

A cucumber is bitter — throw it away. There are briars in the road — turn aside from them. This is enough. Do not add 'and why were such things made in the world?'

BOOK VIII, MEDITATION 50

Meditations on Nature

Whether the universe is a concourse of atoms, or Nature is a system, let this first be established: that I am a part of the whole which is governed by Nature; next, I am in a way intimately related to the parts which are of the same kind as myself. For remembering this, inasmuch as I am a part, I shall be unhappy with nothing that is assigned to me out of the whole; for nothing is injurious to the part, if it is for the advantage of the whole. The whole contains nothing which is not its advantage; and all natures indeed have this common principle, but the nature of the universe has this principle besides, that it cannot be compelled even by any external cause to generate anything harmful to itself. By remembering then, that I am a part of such a whole, I will be content with everything that happens. And inasmuch as I am in a way intimately related to the parts which are of the same kind as myself, I will do nothing antisocial, but will rather direct myself to the things which are of the same kind with myself, and I shall turn all my efforts to the common interest, and divert them from the contrary. Now, if these things are done so, life must flow on happily, just as you may observe that the life of a citizen who continues a course of action which is advantageous to their fellow-citizens is happy, and is content with whatever the state may assign them.

BOOK X, MEDITATION 6

Meditations on Nature

Did Nature herself design to do evil to things which are parts of herself, and to make them subject to evil and of necessity fall into evil, or have such results happened without her knowing it? These suppositions, indeed, are incredible. But if someone should drop the term Nature (as an efficient power), and should speak of these things as natural, even then it would be ridiculous to affirm that parts of the whole are in their nature subject to change, and at the same time to be surprised or vexed as if something were happening contrary to Nature, particularly as the dissolution of things is into those things of which each thing is composed. For there is either a dispersion to the elements out of which everything has been compounded, or a change from the solid to the earthy and from the airy to the aerial, so that these parts are taken back into the universal reason, whether this at certain periods is consumed by fire or renewed by eternal changes.

BOOK X, MEDITATION 7

CHAPTER 5

Meditations on the Gods

Ancient Stoicism was as much a religion as a philosophic school, in that it gave its adherents a framework for thinking about, and connecting to, the divine. The Stoics were convinced that the gods, or God – a singular noun is often preferred to the plural, as seen throughout *Meditations* – are supremely good and closely involved in the world and in human life. In this the Stoics set themselves strongly apart from their chief rival school, the Epicureans, who thought of the gods as remote, disinterested and practically non-existent. Marcus is at pains to refute this view, as seen at 12.28, where the people who ask 'Where have you seen the gods?' are clearly the Epicureans. (Marcus' reply to the challenge, 'They can be seen with the eyes', is somewhat opaque but may refer to the stars and heavenly bodies, regarded by him as divinities.)

Entry 9.28 presents another stark contrast between Stoic and Epicurean worldviews. For the Stoics, the benevolence of the gods takes the form of a continuing plan for the universe and for humanity ('the universal motion puts itself in motion for each individual effect'). The Epicureans by contrast thought that the gods had first set the cosmos running but then withdrew from it, leaving the movements of atoms and their unpredictable 'swerves' to randomly determine the course of events. Marcus firmly believes in the Stoic model, but he also has advice for those who do not: 'If chance rules, do not also be governed by it'; keep to a moral purpose even if you think the universe has none.

In a very few passages of *Meditations*, such as 6.43, Marcus speaks of traditional gods like Asclepius and 'the fruit-bearer' (Demeter, or Ceres as she was called by the Romans). In general, though, he avoids anthropomorphism. In his view the divine is cosmic in scope, coextensive perhaps with the cosmos itself. It is closely identified with Logos, Reason, sometimes described as 'commanding' or seen as the force which directs the universe. Each person's reasoning mind is a splinter of this vast entity and a small incarnation of it, as seen in 12.26 in the previous section: 'Everyone's intelligence is a god.' But the divine is also seen as external, such that it can, and should, be worshipped and prayed to.

A world without gods was unthinkable to Marcus, for the gods, in his view, give meaning to all existence. 'Everything – a horse, a vine – exists for a reason,' he says (8.19), implying that all creation takes part in the divinely arranged scheme of cause and effect. Each living thing has its part to play in the cosmic web (10.8). Human beings play our part by revering the gods and striving, through cultivation of virtue, to become like them. Thanks to the sparks of divinity within us, our reasoning minds, we can make contact with the divine and it can make contact with us: God 'touches the intelligence only which has flowed and been derived from himself into these bodies' (12.2).

Meditations on the Gods

Behave in a social spirit towards human beings, as they have reason. And on all occasions, call upon the gods

BOOK VI, MEDITATION 23

The periodic movements of the universe are the same, up and down, from age to age

BOOK IX, MEDITATION 28

Everything – a horse, a vine – exists for a reason. Why do you wonder? Even the sun will say, 'I am for a purpose', and the rest of the gods will say the same

BOOK VIII, MEDITATION 19

Meditations on the Gods

Either the universal intelligence puts itself in motion for each individual effect, and if this is so, be content with the result of its activity. Or it put itself in motion just once, and everything else has followed in a sequence. Or, indivisible elements are the origin of all things. Put simply, if there is a god, all is well, and if chance rules, do not also be governed by it. Soon the earth will cover us all, then the earth too will change, and the results of that change will change again, and so it will continue forever. If we reflect on all the alterations and transformations which follow one another, wave after wave, we will come to despise everything that is perishable.

BOOK IX, MEDITATION 28

The gods either have power, or they do not. If they have no power, why do you pray to them? But if they do have power, why don't you instead ask to not fear the things you fear, or not desire the things you desire, or not be pained by anything, rather than praying that any particular thing should or shouldn't happen? For if the gods cooperate with people, they can certainly cooperate for these purposes. But perhaps you will say, the gods have placed them in your power. Well then, is it not better to use what is in your power like someone who is free, rather than desiring in a slavish, abject way that which is not yours? And who says that the gods do not aid us even in the things which are in our power? Begin, then, to pray in this way, and you will see. One man prays: how can I sleep with that woman? Instead he should pray: how can I stop desiring her? Another person prays: how can I escape this situation? Instead they should pray: how can I stop wanting to escape? And finally, another prays: please don't let me lose my little child. Instead they should pray: how shall I not be afraid of loss? Turn your prayers this way, and see what comes.

BOOK IX, MEDITATION 40

Meditations on the Gods

It will greatly help you, if you remember the gods, and that they wish not to be flattered, but wish all rational beings to be made like themselves; if you remember that a fig tree does the work of a fig tree, a dog does the work of a dog, a bee does a work of a bee, and a human does the work of a human.

BOOK IX, MEDITATION 9

God sees the minds of all people bared of the material vesture, rind and impurities. For with his intellectual part alone he touches the intelligence only which has flowed and been derived from himself into these bodies. And if you also use yourself to do this, you will rid yourself of much trouble.

BOOK XI, MEDITATION 2

Take care to not become a Caesar, that you are not dyed with that dye; it can happen. Keep yourself simple, good, pure, serious, unpretentious, a friend of justice, a worshipper of the gods, kind and strenuous in all that you do

BOOK VI, MEDITATION 30

To those who ask, 'Where have you seen the gods? How do you know they exist and so worship them?', I answer, 'They can be seen with the eyes. But consider, I have never seen my own soul and yet I honour it'

BOOK XII, MEDITATION 28

Adorn yourself with simplicity and modesty and with indifference towards the things which lie between virtue and vice. Love humanity. Follow god

BOOK VII, MEDITATION 31

Meditations on the Gods

Here are the things peculiar to the good person: to be pleased and content with what happens and with their fate; to not defile the divinity planted within them, nor disturb it by a crowd of images, but to preserve it tranquil, following it obediently as a god, never lying or doing anything unjust. And if all people refuse to believe that this person lives a simple, modest and contented life, they are neither angry nor do they deviate from the way which leads to the end of life, to which a person ought to come pure, tranquil, ready to depart and without any compulsion perfectly reconciled to their lot.

BOOK III, MEDITATION 16

There is only one fruit in this earthly life: a pious disposition and social acts. Do everything as a disciple of Antoninus. Remember his constancy; his reason, evenness, piety, serenity of countenance, sweetness, his disregard of empty fame and his efforts to understand things. He would never let anything pass without carefully examining and clearly understanding it. He bore with those who blamed him unjustly without blaming them in return, he did nothing in a hurry and he didn't listen to slander. He was an exact examiner of manners and actions, he wasn't given to reproach and he wasn't timid, suspicious or a sophist. He was satisfied with so little in terms of lodging, bed, dress, food and servants, and he was laborious and patient ... Imitate all this in order to have as a good a conscience as he did, when your last hour comes.

BOOK VI, MEDITATION 30

If you view things outside of your power as either good or evil, if such a bad thing occurs, or such a good thing is lost, you will certainly blame the gods and hate people too: those who are the real or suspected cause of the misfortune. Indeed, we do much injustice, because we do not see such things as indifferent. But if we judge only those things which are in our power to be good or bad, there is no reason either for finding fault with god or being hostile to humanity.

BOOK VI, MEDITATION 41

Does the sun do the work of the rain, or Aesculapius the work of the fruit-bearer? And how is it with the stars? Are they not each different and yet working together to the same end?

BOOK VI, MEDITATION 43

CHAPTER 6

Meditations on Compassion

Love of one's neighbour is a Christian ethical goal, but also one espoused by Marcus (11.1) and other Stoic thinkers. Indeed, early Christians took many of their guiding principles from the Stoics. Both groups believed in the essential unity of the human race and emphasised the mutual obligations among its members, in contrast to older schools of thought that stressed rights and distinctions. Marcus' injunction to himself, 'love humanity' (7.31, page 117), sounds like something Jesus might have told his disciples. But Marcus also makes clear at various points the difficulty of carrying out this programme. His patience is constantly tried by those who impede, insult or offend him, even by those with bad breath or body odour (5.28). He shows us, in a way Jesus does not, the effort it takes to extend universal love: 'I must do good to people and endure them' (5.20).

Marcus fortifies his compassion with a variety of mental exercises (one entry in *Meditations*, given in part below [11.18], lists nine of these). One is to remind himself that those who do wrong are acting not out of malice but out of ignorance of the good. 'Everyone who misses their object is gone astray,' he reminds himself (9.42). It's proper to pity such people (7.26), or even to instruct them on how to be better. At 11.18 he shows us how such instruction might play out: he imagines telling a violent attacker that he is only harming himself, and that 'even bees do not do as they do.' The point is that humans, like bees, form an interdependent community, but have the good sense not to harm the whole by harming one of its parts.

Another Stoic practice undergirding Marcus' compassion is his refusal to allow himself to feel wronged. 'How have you been injured?' he imagines asking himself, after becoming irritated (9.42); 'no one ... has done anything by which your mind could be made worse.' If our capacity for reason and virtue remains intact, then, in Stoic terms, we have not been harmed, so there's no call for outrage. In fact it's our own outrage that will harm us, if we allow it to overwhelm our reason.

In a third, typically Stoic exercise, Marcus reminds himself that foolish, shameless and annoying people are simply an inescapable part of life; their existence is no more to be resented than that of adverse winds or wild beasts (5.20). Indeed they can be regarded as challenges, opportunities for the Stoic to exercise the virtues of patience and tolerance. Thus Marcus tallies up, among his ethical successes, 'to how many ill-minded folk you have shown a kind disposition' (5.31). With each such compassionate interaction, Marcus has become more fully human, for 'humanity is formed by nature to acts of benevolence' (9.42).

A fourth thought that sustains Marcus in his compassion is stated succinctly at 11.18: 'You too do many wrongs; you are a person like any other.' Or as Jesus put it, let he who is without sin cast the first stone.

To endure is a part of justice, and people do wrong involuntarily; consider how many already, after mutual enmity, suspicion, hatred and fighting, have been stretched dead, reduced to ashes

BOOK IV, MEDITATION 3

Do not be carried along inconsiderately by the appearance of things, but give help to all according to your ability and their fitness. If they should have sustained loss in matters which are indifferent, do not see this as a damage

BOOK V, MEDITATION 36

Preserving your own character, be friendly, benevolent and mild

BOOK X, MEDITATION 36

Meditations on Compassion

When you are offended by someone's shameless conduct, immediately ask yourself, is it possible then, that shameless people should not exist? It is not possible. Do not then require what is impossible. For this person is just another of those shameless people who inevitably exist in the world. Let the same considerations be present to your mind in the case of those who are dishonest, or faithless, or who do wrong of any form, for you will become more kindly disposed towards everyone individually. It is useful to perceive this too, immediately, when the occasion arises, what virtue Nature has given to humanity to oppose every wrongful act. For as an antidote against stupidity she has given mildness, and against another kind of error, some other power. You can always correct by teaching the person who has gone astray; for everyone who misses their object is gone astray. Besides, how have you been injured? No one who irritates you has done anything by which your mind could be made worse; that which is evil and harmful has its foundation only in the mind. And what is harmful or surprising, if an uninstructed person acts like one who is uninstructed? Consider whether you should instead blame yourself, because you did not expect such a person to err. You could have seen it was likely that they would commit this error, but you forgot and are now surprised it has happened. Most of all, when you blame someone for being faithless or ungrateful, turn to yourself. For the fault is clearly your own, whether you trusted that such a person would keep their promise, or when conferring your kindness you did not do so absolutely, nor yet in such a way as to have received from your very act all the profit. For what more do you want when you have done someone a service? Are you not content that you have done something conforming with your nature, or do you seek to be paid for it? Just as if the eye demanded a recompense for seeing, or the feet for walking. For as these members are formed for a particular purpose, and by working according to their several constitutions obtain what is their own, so also as humanity is formed by Nature to acts of benevolence, when one does anything benevolent or in any other way conducive to the common interest, they have acted conformably to their own constitution, and he gets what is their own.

BOOK IX, MEDITATION 42

Meditations on Compassion

When someone has wronged you, immediately consider with what opinion about good or evil they have done wrong. For when you have seen this, you will pity them, and be neither confused nor angry

BOOK VII, MEDITATION 26

When someone blames or hates you, or another says something injurious, consider what kind of people they really are. You will find no reason to be bothered by their opinions. View them kindly, as friends, for the gods help them too, through dreams and signs

BOOK IX, MEDITATION 27

Meditations on Compassion

In one respect humanity is the nearest thing to me, so far as I must do good to people and endure them. But so far as some make themselves obstacles to my proper acts, people become something indifferent to me, no less than the sun or wind or a wild beast. Now it is true that these may impede my action, but they are no impediments to my affects and disposition, which have the power of acting conditionally and changing. For the mind converts and changes every hindrance to its activity into an aid; so that which is a hindrance is made further to an act, and that which is an obstacle helps us on this road.

BOOK V, MEDITATION 20

Are you angry with the person whose armpits stink? Are you angry with the one whose breath is foul? What good will this anger do you? That person has such breath, and that person has such armpits; it is inevitable that they smell as they do. But they have reason, it may be said, and could realise the issue, if they made the effort. I wish you well of your discovery. Well, you have reason too. Through your own rational faculty you could stir up theirs – show them their error, admonish them. For if they listen, you will cure them, and so there was no need for your anger.

BOOK V, MEDITATION 28

Meditations on Compassion

How have you behaved towards to the gods, your parents, family, children, teachers, to those who looked after you during childhood, to your friends, kinsfolk and your slaves? Consider if you have behaved thus: to have never wronged anyone in deed or word. Remember how many things you have passed through and been able to endure: and that the history of your life is now complete, your service is ended and how many beautiful things you have seen, how many pleasures and pains you have despised, how many things called honourable you have spurned, and to how many ill-minded folks you have shown a kind disposition.

BOOK V, MEDITATION 31

Meditations on Compassion

This too is a property of the rational soul: love of one's neighbour

BOOK XI, MEDITATION I

Meditations on Compassion

You too do many wrongs, you are a person like any other. Even if you abstain from certain faults, you still have the disposition to commit them, either through cowardice, or concern about reputation, or some such mean motive ... Consider that a good disposition is invincible, if it is genuine and not an affected smile, acting a part. For what will the most violent person do to you, if you continue to be kind to them, and if, as opportunity offers, you gently admonish them and calmly correct their errors at the very time they are trying to do you harm, saying 'No, my child: we are formed by Nature for something else: I shall certainly not be injured, but you are injuring yourself.' And show them with gentle tact and by general principles that this is so, and even bees do not do as they do, nor any animals which are formed by Nature to be gregarious.

Meditations on Compassion

And you must do this with neither double meaning nor reproach, but affectionately and without rancour in your soul, not as if you were lecturing them, nor yet that any bystander may admire ... Remember this truth in the excitement of anger: that to be moved by passion is not powerful, but that mildness and gentleness, as they are more agreeable to human nature, so also are they more powerful. Anyone who possesses these qualities possesses strength, nerves and courage, as opposed to the person who is subject to fits of passion and discontent. For in the same degree in which a person's mind is nearer to freedom from all passion, so is it also nearer to power: and as the sense of pain is a characteristic of weakness, so too is anger. If one person yields to pain and another to anger, both are wounded and submit.

BOOK XI, MEDITATION 18

CHAPTER 7
Meditations on Death

Marcus Aurelius was a sickly man, possibly tubercular, and he lived during a difficult era of hardship and uncertainty. A disastrous plague struck the Roman empire, beginning in 166, after Marcus had been in power five years, and continued to rage straight through to the end of his reign in 180. Millions perished of the disease, and Marcus was forced to recruit slaves and gladiators to keep up the strength of his legions. Death was constantly present in his mind. In a grim thought that he quotes from an earlier Stoic, Epictetus, he tells himself: 'You're a little soul carrying around a corpse.'

We have seen in the chapter 'On Nature' that Marcus redefines death as a change of state, involving the disaggregation of our bodily elements. That thought is reiterated at several points below (4.6, 10.7, 4.36, 4.46). Nature requires such dissolution so that new matter can be composed, so death is the converse of birth: 'As you may wait for the time when your child will be born, so be ready for the time when your soul will fall out of this envelope', that is, out of the body (9.3). Marcus nowhere assumes that the soul will have any consciousness after death or retain its individual identity. Most likely he held to the Stoic belief that the soul is reabsorbed into the cosmic intelligence of which it is a small sliver.

The fact that death accords with Nature should be enough in itself to keep us from dreading it, but Marcus goes further and gives us reasons why it should be welcomed. Here, his difficulty in tolerating those around him, discussed in the introduction to 'On Compassion', is on full display. The proximity of people who don't share our principles, he writes at 9.3, makes us long for death, 'lest I too forget myself'. Life among those who lack virtue may cause us to lose our own virtue, a fate worse than death.

At several points in *Meditations* Marcus contemplates the brevity of a single human life as compared with the vast stretch of time that precedes and follows, or its smallness among the multitudes who have lived and died (4.33, 4.50, 4.48). His point is that we should set little value on life and regard its length or brevity as inconsequential. All lives are infinitesimal when set against the life of humankind, even more so that of the cosmos. Marcus casts scorn on life as a way to drive the point home: 'What was yesterday a little mucus' – the semen from which a new life was conceived – 'will tomorrow be a mummy or ashes' (4.48).

All we can do is 'pass through this little space of time in accordance with Nature' (4.48), for a life lived in this way is full no matter how short it may be. Then, as Marcus says in his final sentence, seemingly speaking to himself: 'Depart satisfied, for the one who releases you' – God – 'is also satisfied' (12.36 in the next chapter). ❦

Death is the same as birth, a mystery of Nature: a composition then a decomposition of the same elements

BOOK IV, MEDITATION 5

Many grains of frankincense are on the same altar. One falls first and another later on; it makes no difference

BOOK IV, MEDITATION 15

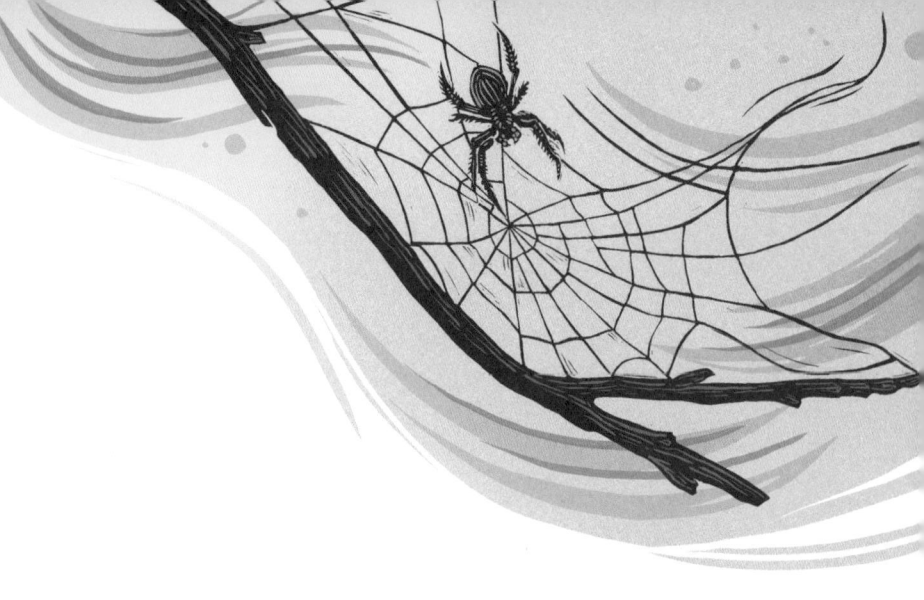

Words which were once familiar are now antiquated: so also the names of those who were famed long ago, are now in a manner antiquated, Camillus, Caeso, Volesus, Leonnatus and a little after also Scipio and Cato, then Augustus, then also Hadrian and Antoninus. For all things soon pass away and become a mere tale, and complete oblivion buries them. And I say this of those who have shone in a wondrous way. For the rest, as soon as they have breathed out their breath, they are gone and no one speaks of them. And, to conclude the matter, what really is an eternal remembrance? A mere nothing. What then is that about which we ought to employ our serious pains? Only this: just thoughts, social acts, honest words and a disposition which gladly accepts all that happens, as necessary, as usual, and flowing from a principle and source of the same kind.

BOOK IV, MEDITATION 33

Meditations on Death

It is a vulgar but still useful help towards contempt of death, to consider those who have tenaciously stuck to life. What more then have they gained than those who have died early? Certainly they lie in their tombs somewhere at last, Cadicianus, Fabius, Julianus, Lepidus and others like them, who have carried out many to be buried, and then were carried out themselves. The interval is small between birth and death; and consider with what trouble, and in company with what sort of people and in what a feeble body this interval is laboriously passed. Do not then consider life a thing of any value. For look to the immensity of time behind you, and to the time which is before you, another boundless space. In this infinity then, what is the difference between the person who lives three days and another who lives three generations?

BOOK IV, MEDITATION 50

Termination of activity, cessation from movement and opinion, and in a sense their death, is no evil. Turn your thoughts now to the consideration of your life as a child, as a youth, your adulthood, your old age, for in these also every change was a death. Is this anything to fear? Turn your thoughts now to your life under your grandfather, then to your life under your mother, then to your life under your father, and as you find many other differences and changes and terminations, ask yourself, is this anything to fear? In like manner then, neither are the termination, cessation and change of your whole life a thing to be afraid of.

BOOK IX, MEDITATION 21

Pass through this little space of time in accordance with Nature and end your journey in peace, as an olive falls when it is ripe, blessing Nature who produced it and thanking the tree on which it grew

BOOK IV, MEDITATION 48

Death is a release from impulsive feelings, from the pulling of strings which move our appetites, from analytical thoughts and from service to the flesh

BOOK VI, MEDITATION 28

No one can escape their destiny. The inquiry should be this: how one can best live in the time they have?

BOOK VII, MEDITATION 46

Meditations on Death

Do not despise death, but be content with it, since it is one of those things which Nature wills. For such as it is to be young and to grow old, to age and reach maturity, to have teeth, a beard and grey hairs, and to conceive, be pregnant and give birth, and all the other natural operations which the seasons of your life will bring, such also is dissolution. This, then, is consistent with the character of a reflecting individual, to be neither careless, impatient nor contemptuous with respect to death, but to wait for it as one of the operations of Nature. As you may wait for the time when your child will be born, so be ready for the time when your soul will fall out of this envelope. But if you also need a vulgar kind of comfort to reach your heart, you will be best reconciled to death by observing the objects from which you will be removed, and the morals of those with whom your soul will no longer be mingled. For it is not right to be offended by others, but it is your duty to care for them and to bear with them gently, and yet to remember that your departure will not be from people who have the same principles as yourself. For this is the only thing, if there be any, which could draw us the contrary way and attach us to life, to be permitted to live with those who have the same principles as ourselves. But now you see how great is the trouble arising from the discordance of those who live together, so you may say, 'Come quick, death, lest I too forget myself.'

BOOK IX, MEDITATION 3

Meditations on Death

All that you see will soon perish, and those who have been spectators of its dissolution will very soon perish too. And the person who dies at the greatest old age will be brought into the same condition with another who died prematurely.

BOOK IX, MEDITATION 33

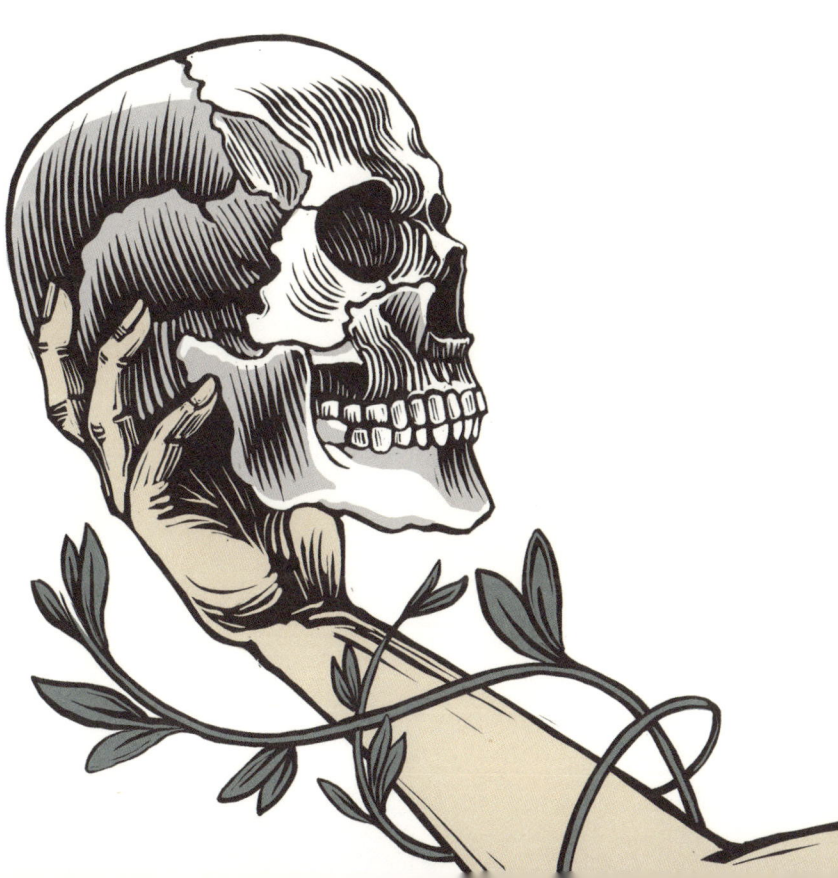

The parts of the whole, everything that forms the natural universe, must of necessity perish, but let this be understood in the sense of undergoing change

BOOK X, MEDITATION 7

Meditations on Death

Everything is only for a day, both that which remembers and that which is remembered.

Observe constantly that all things occur through change, and accustom yourself to consider that the nature of the universe loves nothing so much as to change the things which are and to make new things like them. For everything exists in a manner of the seed of that which will be. You are thinking only of seeds which are cast into the earth or into a womb, but this is a very vulgar notion.

You will soon die, and you are not yet simple, undistracted and without suspicion of being hurt by external things, nor kindly disposed towards all; nor do you yet place wisdom only in acting justly.

BOOK IV, MEDITATIONS 35–37

Meditations on Death

Always remember the saying of Heraclitus, that the death of earth is to become water, the death of water is to become air, and the death of air is to become fire, and reversely. And think too of the person who forgets where a road leads, and that people quarrel with the thing which they are most constantly in communion, the reason which governs the universe; and the things which daily meet with seem to them strange: and consider that we should not act and speak as if we were asleep, for even in sleep we seem to act and speak, and that we should not, like children who learn from their parents, simply act and speak as we have been taught.

If any god told you that you will die tomorrow, or perhaps shortly afterwards, you would not care much whether it be tomorrow or three days from now, unless you were extremely mean-spirited – for how small is the difference! So think it no great thing to die after as many years as you can name rather than tomorrow.

Think continually how many doctors are dead after often frowning over the sick, how many astrologers after predicting with great pretensions the deaths of others and how many philosophers after endless discourses on death or immortality. Think how many heroes are dead after killing thousands, how many tyrants who have used their power over people's lives with terrible insolence as if they were immortal and how many cities are entirely dead, so to speak, Helice, Pompeii, Herculaneum and innumerable others. Add to the reckoning all those who you have known, one after another. One person after burying another has been laid out dead, and another buries them: and all this in a short time. To conclude, always observe how ephemeral and worthless human beings are, and what was yesterday a little mucus will tomorrow be a mummy or ashes.

BOOK IV, MEDITATIONS 46–48

CHAPTER 8
Meditations on Time

At the start of his final notebook, Marcus writes 'Take no notice of the past, trust the future to providence' (12.1; see page 53). He urges himself to focus on the present moment, since that is the only portion of time over which he has influence. His message resonates even more strongly if we assume, as many scholars do, that Marcus was approaching death when he composed the final segment of his *Meditations*. His advice to himself in an earlier phase of the work, to 'make every act of your life as if it were your last' (2.5, page 48) may have been taking on new relevance by this stage.

The present moment, so short that Marcus calls it 'indivisible' (3.10, 5.24), is the only time frame in which we can exercise reason or perform virtuous acts. We distract ourselves from those vital pursuits by looking backwards, often at things we regret, or forwards, at things that cause us fear or anxiety and that are, in any case, already predetermined and out of our control (see the introduction to 'On Living Well'). To be rattled by either the past or the future is the mark of a fool (5.23). If we think of the present as a succession of single moments, we can better cope with any pain or misfortune, for we only have to endure these one second at a time. Thus Marcus tells himself to 'circumscribe' the present (8.36), be fencing it off from what precedes or will follow (just as those in crisis today or suffering from an illness might be told to 'take it day by day').

Marcus often contemplates the vastness of time, and the generations that have lived and died before him, as a way to fathom his own insignificance. A single lifespan is vanishingly small when set in this frame (9.35) and is 'soon swallowed up in the eternal' (12.32). The goals and achievements of those who lived in the time of Vespasian, a century before Marcus wrote, or Trajan, a bit more recent, have entirely passed away, so why should we take our own petty strivings seriously (4.32)? Marcus at one point expresses certainty that he too will be forgotten as the river of time flows onwards. One wonders what he would make of the fact that his *Meditations* are widely read today and his memorial column in Rome, covered in bas-relief scenes of his wars on the northern frontier, is visited by multitudes every year.

Marcus' thoughts about time overlap with his musings on death, examined in the previous section. In his final entry in *Meditations* he imagines each human life as a play to which the cosmic mind has allotted a certain number of acts. We might expect our 'play' to run five acts, the usual length of a tragedy, only to find ourselves kicked off the stage after three. Perhaps Marcus knew, as he wrote those words, his own drama was about to be cut short. He died just shy of his 59th birthday. ❧

Time is like a river, made up of events. It is a violent stream, for as soon as a thing has been seen it is carried away, and another thing comes in its place, which will also be carried away

BOOK IV, MEDITATION 43

A limit of time is fixed for you, and if you do not use it for clearing away the clouds from your mind, it will go, and you will go, and it will never return

BOOK II, MEDITATION 4

Consider that as heaps of sand piled on one another hide the former sands, so in life, the events which go before are soon covered by those which come after

BOOK VII, MEDITATION 34

Every person's life is sufficient. But yours is nearly finished, and yet instead of reverencing your own soul, you place your felicity in the souls of others.

BOOK II, MEDITATION 6

Do external things which happen to you distract you? Give yourself time to learn something new and good, and cease to be whirled around. But you must also avoid being carried the other way. For those who have wearied themselves in life by their activity, and yet have no object to which they can direct every movement, and in a word their thoughts too, are also triflers.

BOOK II, MEDITATION 7

Consider this, which is close to you, the boundless abyss of the past and of the future in which all things disappear. How then is the person who is puffed up with such things or plagued about them to the point of becoming miserable not a fool? For they are bothered only for a time, and a short time.

BOOK 5, MEDITATION 23

Think of the universal substance, of which you have a very small portion, and of universal time, of which a short and indivisible interval has been assigned to you. Think also of that which is fixed by destiny, and how small a part of it you are.

BOOK V, MEDITATION 24

Do not disturb yourself by thinking about the whole duration of your life. Do not let your thoughts at once embrace all the various troubles which you may expect to befall you, but on every occasion ask yourself: what is there in this which is intolerable and unbearable? For you will be ashamed to confess it. In the next place, remember that neither the future nor the past pains you, but only the present. But this is reduced to a very little, if you only circumscribe it, and chide your mind, if it is unable to hold against even this.

BOOK VIII, MEDITATION 36

To put it briefly, your life is short. You must turn the present to profit by the aid of reason and justice

BOOK IV, MEDITATION 26

Bear in mind that every person lives only in this present time, an indivisible point. All the rest of their life is either past or uncertain

BOOK III, MEDITATION 10

Meditations on Time

How quickly all things disappear, in the universe the bodies themselves, but in time, the remembrance of them. What is the nature of all sensible things, and particularly those which attract with the bait of pleasure or which terrify by pain, or are noised abroad by vapoury fame; how worthless, contemptible, sordid, perishable and dead they are – all this, it is the part of the intellectual faculty to observe.

BOOK II, MEDITATION 12

Meditations on Time

The person who has a vehement desire for posthumous fame does not consider that everyone who will remember them will themselves also die very soon. Then again, also they who have succeeded them, until the whole remembrance shall have been extinguished, as it is transmitted through people who foolishly admire and perish. But suppose that those who will remember are immortal, and that the remembrance will be immortal, even then, what is that to you?

BOOK IV, MEDITATION 19

Consider, for example, the time of Vespasian. You will see all these things: people marrying, bringing up children, sickness, death, warring, feasting, trafficking, farming, flattering, obstinate arrogance, suspecting, plotting, death wishes, grumbling, loving, the heaping up of treasure, the desiring of consulships and kingly power. Well then, the life of those people no longer exists at all. Again, remove to the time of Trajan. Again, all is the same. Their life too is gone. In like manner also view the other epochs of time and of whole nations, and see how many after great efforts soon fell and were resolved into the elements. But chiefly you should think of those who you have known distracting themselves about idle things, neglecting to do what was in accordance with their proper constitution, and to hold firmly to this and to be content with it. And here it is necessary to remember that the attention given to everything has its proper value and proportion. For thus you will not be dissatisfied, if you apply yourself to smaller matters no more than is appropriate.

BOOK IV, MEDITATION 32

Look at human things as smoke and nothing at all; reflect especially that what has once changed will never exist again in the infinite duration of time

BOOK X, MEDITATION 31

Meditations on Time

On the occasion of every act, ask yourself, how is this with respect to me? Will I repent of it? A little time and I will be dead, and all is gone. What more do I seek, if what I am now doing is the work of an intelligent living being, and a social being, and one who is under the same law with God?

BOOK VIII, MEDITATION 2

You can move many useless things out of the way among those which disturb you, for they lie entirely in your opinion. You will then gain for yourself ample space by comprehending the whole universe in your mind, and by contemplating the eternity of time, and observing the rapid change of every single thing, how short is the time from birth to dissolution, and the illimitable time before as well as the equally boundless time after dissolution.

BOOK IX, MEDITATION 32

How small a part of the boundless and unfathomable time is assigned to every person? For it is very soon swallowed up in the eternal. And how small a part of the whole substance? And how small a part of the universal soul? And on what a small clod of the whole earth do you walk? Reflecting on all this, consider nothing to be great, except to act as your nature leads you, and to ensure that which the common nature brings.

BOOK XII, MEDITATION 32

Meditations on Time

You have been a citizen in this great state, the world: what difference does it make to you whether that is for five years or three? For that which is conformable to the law is just for all. Where is the hardship then, if it is neither a tyrant not an unjust judge who sends you away from the state, but Nature who brought you into it? The same as if a praetor who has employed an actor dismisses him from the stage. 'But I have not finished the five acts of the play, but only three of them,' you say. But in life three acts can be the whole drama, for what shall be a complete drama is determined by the one who was once the cause of its composition, and now of its dissolution, but you are the cause of neither. Depart satisfied, for the one who releases you is also satisfied.

BOOK XII, MEDITATION 36

FURTHER READING

There are many good English translations of Marcus Aurelius' *Meditations*. Those by George Long (1862), A. S. L. Farquharson (1944), Gregory Hays (2002), Martin Hammond (2006) and Robin Waterfield (2021) are particularly well regarded.

OTHER POPULAR BOOKS ABOUT MARCUS AURELIUS AND STOICISM

Marcus Aurelius: The Stoic Emperor by Donald Robertson (Yale University Press, 2024)

Lives of the Stoics: The Art of Living from Zeno to Marcus Aurelius by Ryan Holiday and Stephen Hanselman (Profile Books, 2020)

Lessons in Stoicism: What Ancient Philosophers Teach Us About How to Live by John Sellars (Allen Lane, 2019)

The Little Book of Stoicism: Timeless Wisdom to Gain Resilience, Confidence and Calmness by Jonas Salzgeber (Jonas Salzgeber, 2019)

How to Think Like a Roman Emperor: The Stoic Philosophy of Marcus Aurelius by Donald Robertson (St Martin's Press, 2019)

Stoicism and the Art of Happiness: Practical Wisdom for Everyday Life by Donald Robertson (Teach Yourself, 2018)

The Daily Stoic: 366 Meditations on Wisdom, Perseverance, and the Art of Living by Ryan Holiday and Stephen Hanselman (Profile Books, 2016)

Marcus Aurelius: A Life by Frank McLynn (Da Capo Press, 2009)

OTHER WORKS ON PHILOSOPHY BY JAMES ROMM

Plato and the Tyrant: The Fall of Greece's Greatest Dynasty and the Making of a Philosophic Masterpiece (Norton, 2025)

How to Have a Life: An Ancient Guide to Using Our Time Wisely (Princeton University Press, 2022)

How to Keep Your Cool: An Ancient Guide to Anger Management (Princeton University Press, 2019)

How to Die: An Ancient Guide to the End of Life (Princeton University Press, 2017)

Dying Every Day: Seneca at the Court of Nero (Random House, 2014)

ABOUT THE CONTRIBUTORS

JAMES ROMM is Professor of Classics at Bard College in Annandale, New York, and the author of several books on the ancient world, including *Dying Every Day: Seneca at the Court of Nero*. His reviews and essays appear regularly in *The Wall Street Journal* and the *London Review of Books*. He is editor of the Ancient Lives series published by Yale University Press.

JOANNA LISOWIEC is an award-winning illustrator and designer. Originally from Poland, she lived in the US and Switzerland before settling in Yorkshire, UK. She is known for her bold style of illustration, which often focuses on the beauty of nature and narratives inspired by folklore. She holds degrees from Edinburgh College of Art and the University of Leeds.